For my Mama,
Thank you for giving me the gift of my voice,
one bedtime song at a time.

Copyright © 2023 by Amanda Esch-Cormier

All rights reserved.

No part of this publication may be reproduced, distributed, or transmitted in any form or by any means, including photocopying, recording, or other electronic or mechanical methods, without the prior written permission of the publisher, except as permitted by U.S. copyright law. For permission requests, contact Little Adventures Press or Amanda Esch-Cormier, amandaeschcormier@gmail.com.

The story, all names, characters, and incidents portrayed in this production are fictitious. No identification with actual persons (living or deceased), places, buildings, and products is intended or should be inferred.

Book Cover by Naya Kirichenko

Illustrations by Naya Kirichenko

Every night while I lay down in bed, my mama sings.
She sings songs that swirl all around my head.

She sings of my family and her aunt before her who sang about life and how precious things were.

She sings high and sings low.
She sings fast and sings slow.

Melodies I recognize and some that I don't.
Songs from the radio, songs from church.

She sings when she's happy and the notes twinkle mid-air.
And when she's sad, it feels quiet like a prayer.

Mama sings to the mountains, she sings to the trees.
Mama sings to the birds and then to the bees.

Then one day her voice becomes mine.

I sing it out loud at magical times.

Stronger and stronger my little voice grows.
It grows and grows into a sound of my own.

I sing when I'm happy, I sing when I'm sad.
I sing even though my sister says it sounds really bad.

I sing to the river, I sing to the sea.
I sing for my mama, I sing for me.

My voice is my family.
Their stories, their songs.
It helps me remember where I truly belong.

About the writer

Amanda Esch-Cormier is an experienced educator, children's writer, singer, songwriter, mother, and advocate.
Amanda spent years as a teacher for students with disabilities, specializing in children needing behavioral support.
Through this work, she fell in love with finding innovative ways to break down and retell stories to increase readability, comprehension, as well as, promote empathy and confidence in the classroom.

When she isn't writing, Amanda loves to sing, be out in nature, garden, hang out with friends and family, meet new people, and explore. She lives with her husband, two daughters, and their pets, Izzy, Jolene, and Dolly. Amanda is almost always the first one out on the dance floor.

You can find her @amandaeschcormier on most social media platforms and at www.amandaeschcormier.com

Find other stories by Amanda here:

About the illustrator

Naya Kirichenko is a digital and traditional artist hailing from Ukraine and currently residing in Istanbul, Turkey. She honed her artistic skills through her studies at the esteemed St. Petersburg Stieglitz Art Academy. However, her insatiable thirst for exploration led her to embark on a remarkable journey.

After leaving her formal education, Naya embarked on a nomadic lifestyle, traveling across various countries like Armenia, Georgia, and Turkey. During her travels, she began selling intricately hand-drawn postcards and canvases, immersing herself in the vibrant cultures she encountered.

As fate would have it, Naya's path took an unexpected twist when she discovered the magical world of digital illustration. Embracing this new medium, she embarked on collaborations that brought poetry, children's books, and short stories to life, infusing them with her unique touch.

Ready to be transported into a world of creativity?
Join Naya's artistic journey on Instagram:

◉ **NAYA.ILLUSTRATION**

Made in United States
North Haven, CT
31 October 2024